A chip for me

We dig up the sand
and fill the buckets.

Then we tip them up
and pat the sand.

A gull hops up to us.
He pecks at the sand.

The gull hops up to Dad.
Dad has a chat with him.

We check the rocks
for crabs.

The gull checks the rocks, too. He is on the hunt for a crab.

7

Dan picks up a crab.
He drops it.

The gull grabs the crab.

Dad gets us a box of chicken
and chips for lunch.

The gull is back!

Dad chops up the chicken.
Then we all dig in.

The gull hops on to
Nat's backpack.

Flap, flap,
snap, chomp!

As quick as a wink, the gull
grabs the chip off Dan.

Then a **big plop**
lands on Dan!

Words to blend

buckets	then	flap
pecks	hunt	rocks
picks	crab	just
gull	help	back
snap	wink	quick
backpack		from

Before reading

Synopsis: Dad and the children go to the beach but a seagull is on the hunt for food. It manages to get a chip from Dan and thanks him in a seagull way.

Review phoneme/s: th/th

New phoneme: ch

Story discussion: Look at the cover, and read the title together. Ask: *Who do you think might want a chip? Where do you think this story is set?*

Link to prior learning: Display the grapheme *ch*. Say: *These two letters are a digraph – that means they make one sound together. They make the sound at the start of* chip. Turn to page 10. Can children spot and read three words with *ch*? (chicken, chips, lunch)

Vocabulary check: As quick as a wink – check that children understand this phrase means very quickly indeed. Can they wink or blink very quickly?

Decoding practice: Display the following words with spaces: lun__, __at, __ip, __ops. Ask the children to write in the missing digraph: *ch*. How quickly can they read the finished words?

Tricky word practice: Display the words *you* and *too*. Say the words out loud and ask children what they notice (both words end in the same sound, /oo/). Point out that the letters that make the /oo/ sound are different in both these words. Encourage children to practise writing and reading these words.

After reading

Apply learning: Did the children guess that the gull might try to steal a chip? Did anyone guess what would happen to Dan at the very end of the story?

Comprehension

- What did the children eat in this story? What did the gull eat?

- Which do you think was the funniest part of the story? Why?

- How do you think Dan felt about the gull at the end of the story?

Fluency

- Pick a page that most of the group read quite easily. Ask them to reread it with pace and expression. Model how to do this if necessary.

- Ask children to practise reading the speech bubbles on pages 15 and 16. Can they make it sound as if the characters are really talking?

- Practise reading the words on page 17.

Tricky words review

for	me	we
the	to	he
I	her	you
too	of	all
my	be	she